SCIENCE IN YOUR BACKYARD

by William R. Wellnitz, Ph.D.
Photography by Valerie Spratlin
Illustrations by Shane Meador

TAB BOOKS
Blue Ridge Summit, PA

FIRST EDITION
FIRST PRINTING

Library of Congress Cataloging-in-Publication Data

Wellnitz, William R., 1949-
    Science in your backyard / by William R. Wellnitz.
        p. cm.
    Includes index.

    Summary: Includes experiments involving plants, animals, and earth
sciences that can be done close to home and that encourage the
development of observation and measurement skills.
    ISBN 0-8306-2495-3 (h)   ISBN 0-8306-2495-5 (p)
    1. Science—Juvenile literature. 2. Science—Experiments—
Juvenile literature. 3. Animals—Experiments—Juvenile literature.
4. Plants—Experiments—Juvenile literature. 5. Earth sciences—
—Experiments—Juvenile literature. [1. Science—Experiments.
2. Animals—Experiments. 3. Plants—Experiments. 4. Earth
sciences—Experiments. 5. Experiments.] I. Title.
Q163.W423   1991
507'.6—dc20   91-25117
                                                  CIP
                                                      AC

TAB Books offers software for sale. For information and a catalog, please contact
TAB Software Department, Blue Ridge Summit, PA 17294-0850.

Acquisitions Editor: Kimberly Tabor
Book Editor: Molly Jackel
Production: Katherine G. Brown
Book Design: Jaclyn J. Boone
Cover Photo: Susan Riley, Harrisonburg, VA
Cover Design: Holberg Design, York, PA

Contents

Part III Earth Science Experiments 83

*Experiments ideally suited for science fair projects.

Acknowledgments

I am grateful to Kim Tabor of TAB Books for suggesting this project, and Jane Millward for typing part of the manuscript. It is again a true pleasure to recognize Valerie Spratlin for her photographs, my son Shane Meador for the illustrations, and my daughter Cassie Meador and my son Joshua Wellnitz for serving as models. Finally, my wife Dianne deserves a special thanks for her support during this project.

A Note to Children

Your yard can become your own science laboratory. By using all your senses and a few things found in your home, you can learn many things about the wonders of nature.

Some of the experiments require little or no time and are almost like magic. But they are not magic. They are based on the rules of science. Other experiments go on for many days or weeks, and you must often do something each day. You will need to be patient because not everything happens quickly. Some scientists who study plants or animals work many years to get one result!

The library or bookstore has many excellent books about plants and animals. You may want to check out some books to help you identify trees, birds, plants, or insects.

Look through the book and choose one or two experiments you find interesting. Each experiment tells you at the start what happens. Gather all of the materials you will need for the experiment before you begin, and keep them in one place.

Read the procedure next, but do not read the explanation until you have done the experiment. You are now ready to do the experiment. Follow the directions exactly as they are written. You can look at the pictures to see if you have set up things correctly.

Use all of your senses as you observe what happens. If you must write something down, do so as soon as you make the measurement or observation. Your memory is often not as good as it seems.

Try to figure out what happened during the experiment and why. You might want to repeat the experiment one or two more times to be sure you understand. You can then look at the explanation to see if you figured it out correctly. Try to talk about the experiment with an adult. After you have done the experiment, try changing some of the materials and experiment on your own. Be curious! Have fun!

If you have questions, or if you've done some new and interesting things, or would just like to comment on the book, please write to me: Dr. Bill Wellnitz, Biology Department, Augusta College, Augusta, Georgia 30910.

A Note to Adults

The intent of this book is threefold: 1) to make children aware of the natural world around them; 2) to develop observation and thinking skills in children, and; 3) to show children how scientists actually do their experiments. Many of the experiments in this book have been simplified from actual published experiments.

The experiments in this book often require that the child work or observe each day. You may find it necessary to remind the child that something needs to be done. Children are apt to grow impatient when they do not see results immediately. Encourage their patience, and remind them that growth does not occur immediately. Discussing the time course for the development of a baby is a good way to demonstrate how long certain processes take.

Although most of the experiments can be done by children alone, I encourage you to become involved, but only as a guide. A few experiments demand your assistance and should not be done by children alone. These experiments require use of matches, the stove, or a knife and are clearly indicated by a warning symbol. Help them find the materials, but let them do the experiment themselves. Discuss the results with them, and encourage them to think of explanations and other uses of the process involved.

Two important aspects of science are observation and measurement. Encourage your children to use all of their senses, in order to measure accurately, and to record their observations. For some experiments, I have provided graphs to show children how to present results.

Many of the experiments are intentionally open-ended. Children are naturally curious and will want to vary the procedure or try different materials. Don't become alarmed if they do this, just make certain that on their first attempt they do the experiment as written. Many a great discovery has come from someone modifying an existing procedure.

Some of the explanations provide only a general principle, not the specific result the child will get. In many cases, the results will depend on what materials are used.

The experiments in this book provide a solid background in scientific principles and methodology, and the techniques can easily be applied to other situations. Many of the experiments are ideally suited for science fair projects and these experiments are indicated by an asterisk (*) in the table of contents. If your child does a science fair project, be sure he or she, not you, does the work.

Finally, you might enjoy many of the experiments, and if you have a phobia of science, you too might discover that science can be fun. I welcome your comments about the book, and my address appears in A Note to Children.

Symbols Used in This Book

Some of the experiments used in this book require the use of sharp objects or flame. It is recommended that a parent or teacher supervise young children and instruct them.

All of the experiments in this book can be done safely, but young children should be instructed to respect the lives of small animals and insects and should be made aware of the hazards associated with carelessness. The following symbols can be seen at the beginning of each chapter and are for you to use as a guide to what children might be able to do independently, and what they *should not do* without adult supervision. Keep in mind that some children might not be mature enough to do any of the experiments without adult help, and that these symbols should be used as a guide only, and do not replace the good judgment of parents or teachers.

 Materials or tools used in this experiment could be dangerous in young hands. Adult supervision is recommended. Children should be instructed on the care and handling of sharp tools or conbustible or toxic materials and how to protect surfaces.

 Flame is used in this project and adult supervision is required. Do not wear loose clothing. Tie hair back. When handling candles, wear protective gloves—hot wax can burn. Never leave a flame unattended. Extinguish flame properly. Protect surfaces beneath burning candles.

 The use of the stove, boiling water, or other hot materials are used in this project and adult supervision is required. Keep other small children away from boiling water and burners.

 Electricity is used in this experiment. Young children should be supervised and older children cautioned about the hazards of electricity.

Disclaimer

Ethical science practices involve very careful consideration of living organisms. One cannot recklessly cause pain, damage, or death to any living organism.

Adult supervision is advised when working with these projects. No responsibility is implied or taken for anyone who sustains injuries as a result of using the materials or ideas put forward in this book. Be sure children:

- Taste nothing.
- Use proper equipment (gloves, safety glasses, and other safety precautions).
- Clean up broken glass with a dust pan and brush.
- Use chemicals with extra care.
- Wash hands after project work is done.
- Tie up loose hair and clothing.
- Follow step-by-step procedures; avoid short cuts.
- Never work alone.

Safety precautions are addressed in the text. If you use common sense and make safety the first consideration, you will create safe, fun, educational, and rewarding projects.

Part 1
Animal
Experiments

Animals are living things that usually can move but cannot make their own food; they have to eat plants or other animals for food. Animals can be found almost anywhere: on the ground, in the air, or in the water. Many animals reproduce by laying eggs, but some animals give birth to live young.

Animals are divided into two main groups: those with backbones, and those without backbones.

Below are some of the kinds of animals that you're likely to find or see.

insects	animals with six legs and hard outer shell
spiders	animals with eight legs and hard outer shell
birds	animals with feathers
amphibians	animals that can live both on land and in water
mammals	animals with fur or hair
worms	animals shaped like long tubes

1

Watching Ants

Materials

- BREAD CRUMBS, OR PIECE OF CANDY, OR SMALL PIECE OF MEAT

You will observe the behavior of ants after they discover food. This experiment may take 1 to 2 hours.

PROCEDURE

1. Place the piece of food outside where you can watch it. The sidewalk is often a good place (Fig. 1-1).

2. Look at the food every 5 minutes until ants appear. How long did it take them to find the food?

3. As ants begin to appear, watch them patiently for the next 30 minutes. Do more ants appear?

4. Watch the ants try to carry the food back to their anthill.

Fig. 1-1. *Watching ants on bread.*

COMMENTS

Each anthill always has a few ants out looking for food. When they find food, they go back to the hill to get more ants. The scouts leave a chemical trail that other ants can follow to the food. The other ants will move along this trail. Ants are very strong for their size. They can carry food that is 5 to 10 times heavier than they are.

2
Making a Bird Feeder

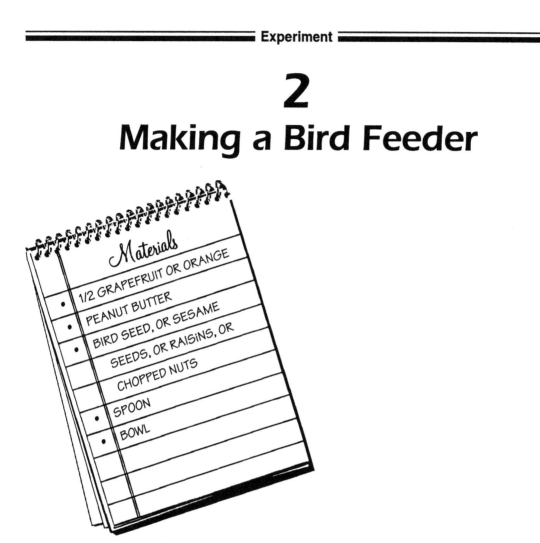

Materials

- 1/2 GRAPEFRUIT OR ORANGE
- PEANUT BUTTER
- BIRD SEED, OR SESAME SEEDS, OR RAISINS, OR CHOPPED NUTS
- SPOON
- BOWL

You can easily make a bird feeder from things in your kitchen.

PROCEDURE

1. Remove the fruit from the grapefruit so that only the peel remains.

2. In a bowl, mix the peanut butter and the seeds or raisins.

3. Use a spoon to fill the grapefruit with the peanut butter mixture (Fig. 2-1).

4. Nail the grapefruit to a tree, or place it on a branch in a bush.

5. Watch to see what kinds of birds come to your feeder.

Fig. 2-1. *Filling a grapefruit with bird seed.*

COMMENTS

Watching birds can be very interesting. You will probably see many different kinds of birds at your feeder. Get a bird book and try to identify the birds.

If you put out food all year, you will probably see different birds at different seasons. Some birds migrate, or move, as the seasons change. In the winter, birds have a difficult time finding food. A bird feeder in the winter will help them get food.

3
What Lives in Soil?

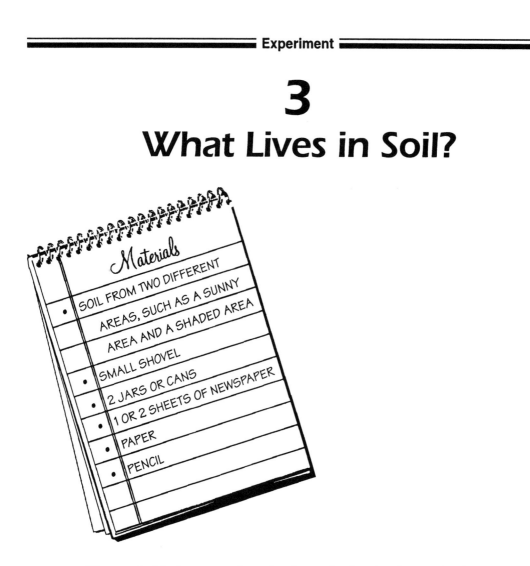

Materials

- SOIL FROM TWO DIFFERENT AREAS, SUCH AS A SUNNY AREA AND A SHADED AREA
- SMALL SHOVEL
- 2 JARS OR CANS
- 1 OR 2 SHEETS OF NEWSPAPER
- PAPER
- PENCIL

You probably have not thought about the kinds of animals that live in the soil. In this experiment you will try to find animals in the soil.

PROCEDURE

1. Pick two different areas to use for your soil. Sunny and shady areas are fine. Areas with two different types of soil such as sand and clay, are even better.

2. Use the shovel to fill the containers with dirt. Try to dig down 3 to 5 inches (7 to 12 cm).

3. Pour the soil onto the newspaper. Spread out the soil.

4. Look for different kinds of animals (Fig. 3-1).

5. Make a list of how many different animals you see. Which soil had the most animals? Use a chart like the one in Fig. 3-2 to record your observations.

Fig. 3-1. *Examining soil for animals.*

Number

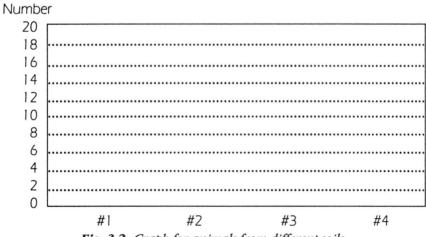

Fig. 3-2. *Graph for animals from different soils.*

EXPLANATION

Different types of soil provide different types of food. Some animals might live in one place but not in another.

4
What Lives in Water?

Materials

- JAR
- FUNNEL (OPTIONAL)
- COFFEE FILTER (OPTIONAL)
- MICROSCOPE OR MAGNIFYING GLASS (OPTIONAL)
- SOURCE OF POND WATER

You will see that pond water has many small animals living in it.

PROCEDURE

1. Use the jar to get some pond water (Fig. 4-1).

2. Look at the water to determine if any animals are living in it.

3. If you have a funnel and a coffee filter, pour the water through the filter. Do this outside or over the sink (Fig. 4-2).

4. Look for animals on the filter. If you find any, look at them with a magnifying glass or microscope.

Fig. 4-1. *Collecting pond water.*

Fig. 4-2. *Pouring pond water through a filter.*

COMMENTS

Some animals live in water. Other animals live in the water only when they are young. Make a list of how many animals you saw.

5
Catching Tadpoles

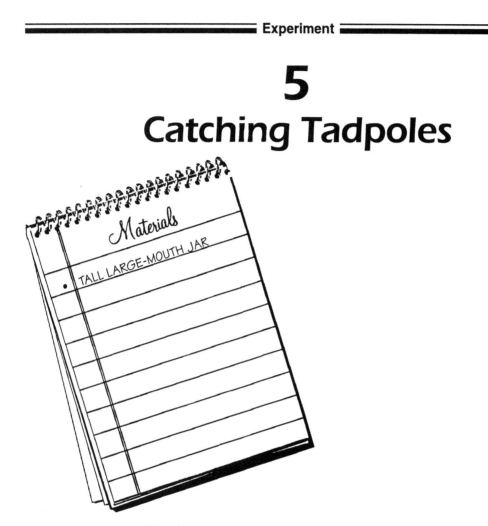

Materials

• TALL LARGE-MOUTH JAR

Spring and early summer are good times to collect tadpoles and to follow their growth. This experiment will take many weeks.

PROCEDURE

1. Find a shallow pond or puddle that has some tadpoles in it.

2. Catch some tadpoles in the jar (Fig. 5-1). Do not put too much water into the jar. A depth of 1 to 2 inches (2.5 to 5.0 cm) is fine (Fig. 5-2).

3. To keep the tadpoles alive and growing, change the water every 2 to 3 days. Use pond water, not tap water.

4. Examine how the tadpoles change (Fig. 5-3).

Fig. 5-1. Collecting tadpoles.

Fig. 5-2. Keep the tadpole in 1 or 2 inches of water.

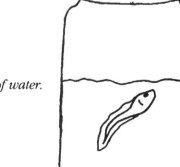

Fig. 5-3. *Stages of frog development.*

COMMENTS

A female frog lays hundreds of eggs. These eggs develop into tadpoles, animals that look more like fish than frogs. As the tadpoles grow in size, they begin to grow legs, and the tail disappears. The animal now looks like a frog.

Only a few tadpoles survive to become frogs. Some tadpoles die, but many are eaten by other animals.

It is important to use pond water to keep the tadpoles alive. Pond water contains many small plants that the tadpoles use for food.

6
What Attracts Butterflies?

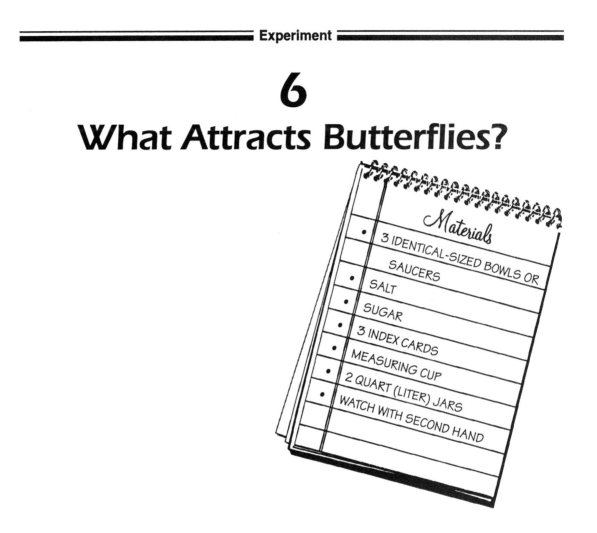

Materials

- 3 IDENTICAL-SIZED BOWLS OR SAUCERS
- SALT
- SUGAR
- 3 INDEX CARDS
- MEASURING CUP
- 2 QUART (LITER) JARS
- WATCH WITH SECOND HAND

You will see what kind of *solution* attracts butterflies. This experiment may take a few hours.

PROCEDURE

1. Mix 1 teaspoon of salt with 1 quart of (liter) of water. Put this solution into a jar labeled "salt."

2. Mix 1 teaspoon of sugar with 1 quart (liter) of water. Put this solution into a jar labeled "sugar."

3. Place three saucers outside where there are some butterflies.

4. Label the saucers "water," "salt," and "sugar" (Fig. 6-1).

5. Fill each saucer with the right solution.

6. When a butterfly (or a bee) comes to one of the saucers, time how long it stays.

7. If a butterfly returns or changes saucers, time how long it stays at the next saucer. At which solution did the butterfly spend the most time?

Fig. 6-1. *Label bowls with "salt," "sugar," and "water."*

COMMENTS

Butterflies seem to prefer the salt solutions. When scientists discovered this fact, they were surprised. They thought the sugar solution would attract the butterfly the best. The results made them change their prediction.

You also can use this experiment to see which solution attracts ants the best.

7
How Animals React to Light

Materials
- CLEAR PLASTIC TUBE AT LEAST 12 INCHES (30 CM) LONG. AN EMBROIDERY OR MAILING TUBE WILL WORK.
- DIFFERENT ANIMALS—FRUIT FLIES, BEETLES, ETC.
- ALUMINUM FOIL

You will see if an animal is attracted to light. This experiment will take about an hour.

PROCEDURE

1. Catch 2 to 10 animals. If you are growing fruit flies (Experiment 11), use them. A few beetles will also work.

2. Cover one-half of the tube with aluminum foil (Fig. 7-1).

3. Remove the cap at the covered end of the tube.

4. Place animals in the tube and close the end.

5. Place the tube in such a way that the sun or a light shines on the uncovered end.

6. Wait 45 to 60 minutes to see which end, dark or light, has more animals.

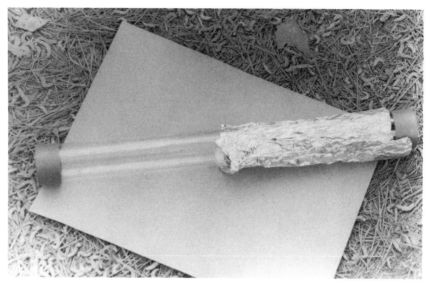

Fig. 7-1. *Cover half the tube with aluminum foil.*

COMMENTS

Some animals like to be in light and will move toward it. Fruit flies are one type of animal that is attracted to light. Other animals, especially those that live in the soil, prefer dark and will move away from the light.

Make a list of animals that are attracted to light and a list of those that are not attracted to light.

8

How Fast Does a Fly Move?

Materials

- JAR WITH LID
- HAMMER AND NAIL
- REFRIGERATOR
- FLY

You will discover how to make a fly move faster or slower. This experiment will take 2 to 3 hours.

PROCEDURE

1. Punch one or two holes in the lid of a jar by hammering a nail through the lid.

2. Use the jar to catch a fly.

3. Put the lid on the jar with the fly inside, and put it in the refrigerator for 30 to 60 minutes.

4. Remove the jar and observe how fast the fly moves (Fig. 8-1).

5. Place the jar outside in the sun for 30 to 40 minutes.

6. Observe how fast the fly now moves.

7. Let the fly out of the jar.

Fig. 8-1. *Watch the movement of the fly in the jar.*

EXPLANATION

The temperature of many animals changes with the outside temperature. Only mammals and birds keep the same temperature. As the temperature of an animal drops, all of the processes in the animal slow down. As a result, animals move more slowly in cold temperatures than in warm temperatures.

9

Mosquito Development

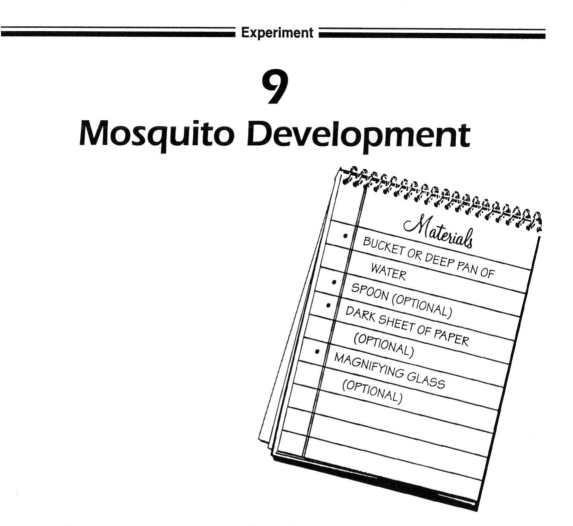

Materials

- BUCKET OR DEEP PAN OF WATER
- SPOON (OPTIONAL)
- DARK SHEET OF PAPER (OPTIONAL)
- MAGNIFYING GLASS (OPTIONAL)

You can raise mosquitoes and watch them grow. This experiment will take 1 to 2 weeks.

PROCEDURE

1. Place bucket of water outside in a shady area.

2. Look at the water each day. At some point you will probably see things crawling or swimming in the water (Fig. 9-1).

3. With a spoon, remove one or two "swimmers" and place them on a dark sheet of paper. What do these "swimmers" look like? (Use a magnifying glass if you have one.)

Fig. 9-1. *Looking for mosquito larvae.*

4. After these animals appear, cover the bucket with an old cloth to trap the adult mosquitoes as they develop.

COMMENTS

Many insects pass through different stages of growth. One example of this type of change is the butterfly. It passes from a tiny egg to a caterpillar to a *cocoon* to a butterfly. Insects such as mosquitoes lay their eggs in water. The eggs develop into swimming *larvae* (LAR-VEE, see Glossary), then into adults.

Have you ever noticed how many mosquitoes are around after much rain? Adult mosquitoes need water to make more mosquitoes.

Some kinds of mosquitoes carry disease. Removing standing water helps to control the spread of diseases.

10
Mysterious Appearance of New Life

Materials

- 2 JARS, 8 OUNCES (250 ML) OR LARGER
- 1 RUBBER BAND
- PIECE OF CLOTH LARGE ENOUGH TO COVER THE TOP OF THE JAR
- 2 PIECES OF FOOD SUCH AS STEW BEEF, BANANA, ETC.

Many, many years ago, people thought that animals mysteriously appeared from other nonliving materials. This famous experiment shows that living flies are needed to make more living flies. This experiment will take about 2 weeks.

PROCEDURE

1. Place one piece of food in each jar.

2. Cover one jar with the cloth. Fasten the cloth with the rubber band. Leave the other jar uncovered (Fig. 10-1).

3. Place both jars outside in an area where they won't be disturbed.

4. Look at each jar every day until you see some type of animals in one of the jars.

Fig. 10-1. *Cover one jar with a cloth and rubber band, and leave the other jar open.*

COMMENTS

This experiment is a repeat of the famous experiment first done by Francesco Redi over 300 years ago. In your experiment, *larvae*, or *maggots*, probably appeared in the open jar, but not in the covered jar.

Adult flies entered the open jar, and laid eggs in the food. The eggs hatched, developed first into larvae, then into adult flies.

By keeping one of the jars covered, you prevented flies from laying eggs on the food. From this experiment you can see that life does not appear without preexisting life.

11
Collecting Fruit Flies

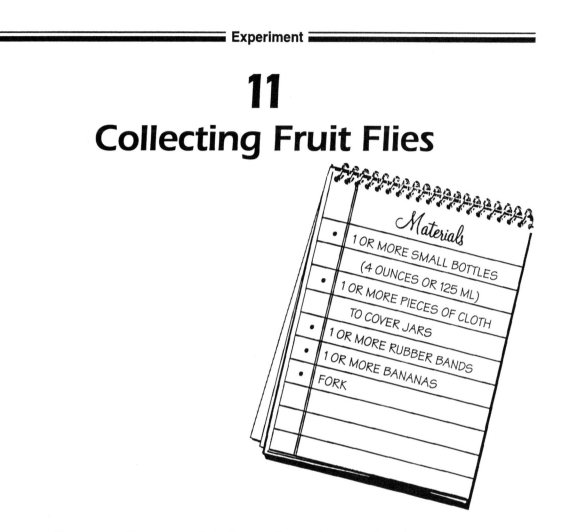

Materials

- 1 OR MORE SMALL BOTTLES (4 OUNCES OR 125 ML)
- 1 OR MORE PIECES OF CLOTH TO COVER JARS
- 1 OR MORE RUBBER BANDS
- 1 OR MORE BANANAS
- FORK

You can collect some fruit flies and use them to do other experiments in this section. This experiment will take about 2 weeks.

PROCEDURE

1. Peel a banana and mash it up with a fork.

2. Put enough mashed banana in a jar to make a 1 inch (2.5 cm) layer.

3. Place the jar outside where it won't be disturbed (Fig. 11-1).

4. Look at the jar every 2 or 3 days.

5. When you see the larvae crawling in the food, or on the sides of the jar, cover the jar with a cloth. Secure the cloth with a rubber band.

6. A few days after you see larvae, flies will appear.

Fig. 11-1. Place the jar of mashed bananas outside.

COMMENTS

Flies, like butterflies and mosquitoes, have different forms at different times of their lives. The adult flies that you have "raised" will produce more young in another 2 weeks. You can now use these flies to do some other experiments (See Experiment 17).

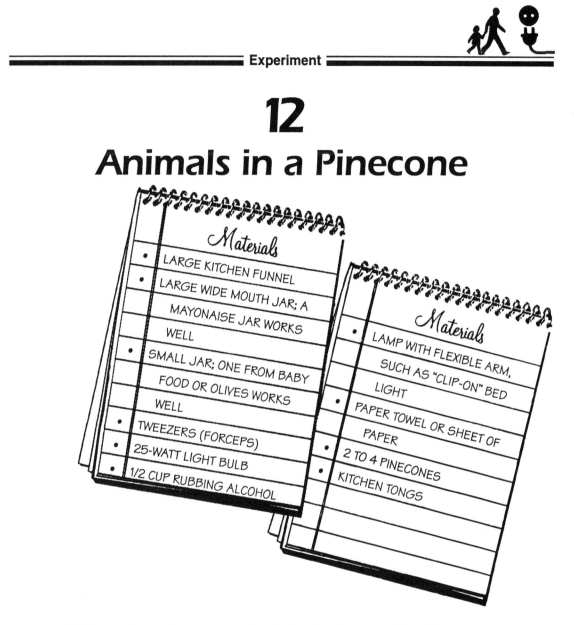
12
Animals in a Pinecone

Materials
- LARGE KITCHEN FUNNEL
- LARGE WIDE MOUTH JAR; A MAYONAISE JAR WORKS WELL
- SMALL JAR; ONE FROM BABY FOOD OR OLIVES WORKS WELL
- TWEEZERS (FORCEPS)
- 25-WATT LIGHT BULB
- 1/2 CUP RUBBING ALCOHOL

Materials
- LAMP WITH FLEXIBLE ARM, SUCH AS "CLIP-ON" BED LIGHT
- PAPER TOWEL OR SHEET OF PAPER
- 2 TO 4 PINECONES
- KITCHEN TONGS

Did you know that many animals live in pinecones? In this experiment you will see what kinds of animals live in a pinecone. This experiment will take about 1 week.

PROCEDURE

1. Fill the small jar one-half full with alcohol. DO NOT TASTE THE ALCOHOL.

2. Using the tongs or tweezers, put the small jar into the large jar.

3. Place the funnel in the large jar. The edge of the funnel should stick over the edge of the jar.

4. Place the pinecones in the funnel.

5. Place the lamp 2 to 4 inches (5 to 10 cm) above the pinecones. (Fig. 12-1).

6. Turn the light on and leave it on for 5 to 7 days.

7. After 5 to 7 days, turn the light off and remove the funnel.

8. Remove the small jar.

9. With tweezers, remove the animals from the jar onto the paper and look at them. If you have a magnifying glass, you might want to use it.

Fig. 12-1. Place the pinecones in a funnel under a lamp.

EXPLANATION

The light heats up the pinecones. The animals move away from the heat and fall into the alcohol. The alcohol kills them. If you want to collect live animals, use a small jar without the alcohol. You might want to repeat this experiment with a different type of pinecone. You may find different animals in the second type of pinecone.

13
Collecting Insects

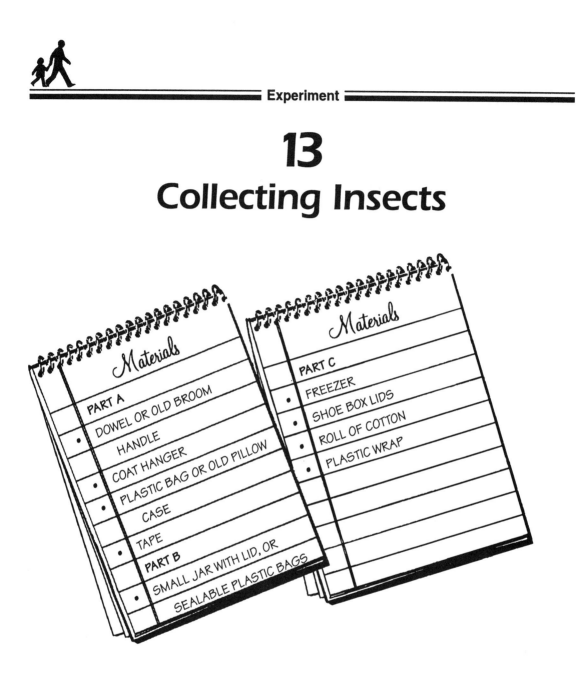

Materials

PART A
- DOWEL OR OLD BROOM HANDLE
- COAT HANGER
- PLASTIC BAG OR OLD PILLOW CASE
- TAPE

PART B
- SMALL JAR WITH LID, OR SEALABLE PLASTIC BAGS

Materials

PART C
- FREEZER
- SHOE BOX LIDS
- ROLL OF COTTON
- PLASTIC WRAP

You will collect, kill, and display insects. This experiment will take 5 to 7 days. It is broken down into parts.

PROCEDURE

Part A—Making an insect net

1. Bend the coat hanger into the shape of a circle.

2. Tape or sew the pillow case or plastic bag to the coat hanger.

3. Straighten the hooked part of the hanger.

4. Attach the hanger to the stick with tape or have an adult drill a hole in the stick for the hanger (Fig. 13-1).

Fig. 13-1. *Make your own insect net.*

Part B—Catching insects

1. Use the net to catch flying insects (Fig. 13-2).

2. When you have an insect in the net, squeeze the end of the net to keep the insect from flying out.

3. Stick the end of the net into the jar or plastic bag so the insect enters the jar (Fig. 13-3).

4. Cover the jar.

5. To catch an insect on the ground, put the jar over the insect. Then lift the jar and quickly put on the lid.

Part C—Killing and displaying insects

1. Get permission from your parent to store insects in the freezer.

2. Put the closed jar or the sealed bag in the freezer. Keep it in the freezer at least two days.

3. Unroll some cotton to line the lid of a shoe box.

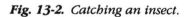
Fig. 13-2. *Catching an insect.*

Fig. 13-3. *Putting an insect in a bag.*

4. Take the insect out of the freezer. Its body should now be soft and flexible.

5. Gently spread the wings and legs to get the position you want.

6. Put the insect on the cotton (Fig. 13-4).

7. Try to identify the insects you caught. See Fig. 13-5 for some of the kinds of insects you might catch.

8. Cover the shoe box with plastic wrap.

Fig. 13-4. *Mount the insects on cotton.*

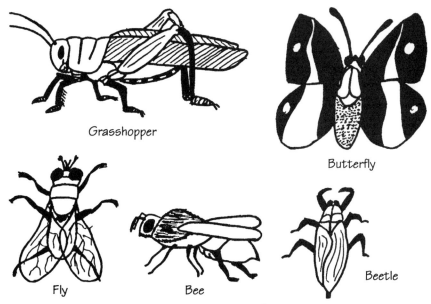

Grasshopper

Butterfly

Fly

Bee

Beetle

Fig. 13-5. *Identify and label the different kinds of insects you catch.*

COMMENTS

You can find insects everywhere: on the ground, in the air, under rocks. There are more insects in the world than any other type of animal. To attract many insects, take an old white sheet or T-shirt and place it outside. One hour later you will probably see many different kinds of insects on the sheet.

You killed the insects by freezing them. This is what happens to adult insects in the winter. New insects appear in the spring because the eggs survived the freezing.

Part II
Plant
Experiments

Plants are wonderful living things. They are the only living things that can use the energy from the sun to make their own food. As plants make their own food, they give off oxygen that we breathe. We could not live long without plants.

Plants start out as a seed. The seed takes in water and swells. This seed then grows into a plant. The new plant has many leaves to catch the sunlight. The plant eventually makes a flower which in turn makes more seeds.

In this chapter you will see how plants grow. You will also find out what things make a plant grow better or worse. You will learn how to identify plants.

14
Making a Leaf Collection

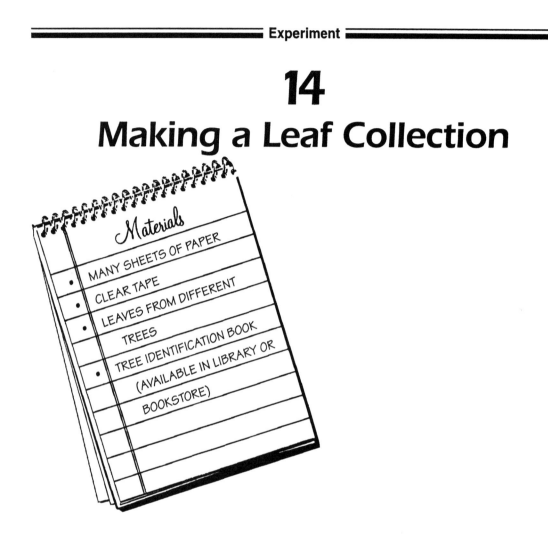

Materials

- MANY SHEETS OF PAPER
- CLEAR TAPE
- LEAVES FROM DIFFERENT TREES
- TREE IDENTIFICATION BOOK (AVAILABLE IN LIBRARY OR BOOKSTORE)

There are probably many different trees in your yard or on your school grounds. You can learn about different kinds of trees by making a leaf collection. This experiment may take several days or weeks.

PROCEDURE

1. Take a leaf from a tree.

2. Tape it to a sheet of paper. Put only one type of leaf on each page (Fig. 14-1).

3. Use the tree book to find out which tree your leaf came from.

4. Write the name of the tree under the leaf.

5. Try to collect many different leaves.

6. To make a more complete collection you can tape a piece of bark and a seed (if you can find one) to the page with the leaf, and use the tree book to identify the tree.

Fig. 14-1. *Mounting a leaf.*

COMMENTS

This experiment will help you recognize trees wherever you find them. The bark and the seed may help you even if the tree has no leaves when you see it. The arrangement and the shape of the leaves will help you identify the plant or tree.

15
Examining Flowers

Materials

DIFFERENT KINDS OF FLOWERS

KNIFE OR RAZOR BLADE

MAGNIFYING GLASS

(OPTIONAL)

You will look at the different parts of a flower.

PROCEDURE

1. Get a flower.

2. Try to identify the male and female parts. (Fig. 15-1). The male parts will make the *pollen* . The female part will make the seeds.

3. Ask an adult to cut open the bottom of the female part so you can see the seeds (Fig. 15-2).

4. If you have a magnifying glass, use it to look at the different parts of the flower.

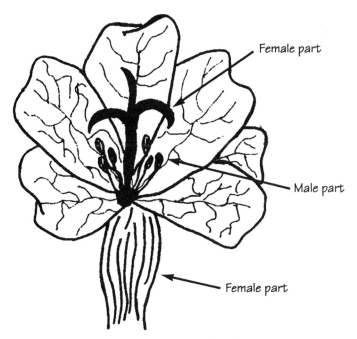

Female part

Male part

Female part

Fig. 15-1. *Parts of a flower.*

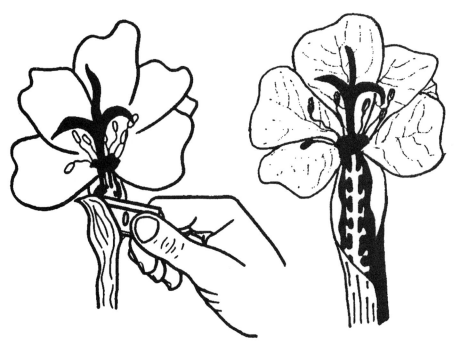

Fig. 15-2. *Have an adult open the female part.*

COMMENTS

Some flowers will have only male or only female parts. Notice that in flowers with both male and female parts, the female part is always higher than the male part. The reason the female part of the flower is higher is so that the pollen, which usually comes from a different flower, can easily fall down into the female part..

The female part usually makes a sweet *nectar* to attract birds or insects. When the insect gets some nectar, some of the pollen sticks to its wings or legs. When it flies to another flower, some of the pollen falls onto the female part. The pollen travels down the long tube and helps to make a seed.

Try to figure out what kind of animal is attracted to a certain kind of flower. Insects, especially bees and butterflies, are very important to farmers. These insects help the plants to make the fruits and vegetables.

16
Examining Mosses

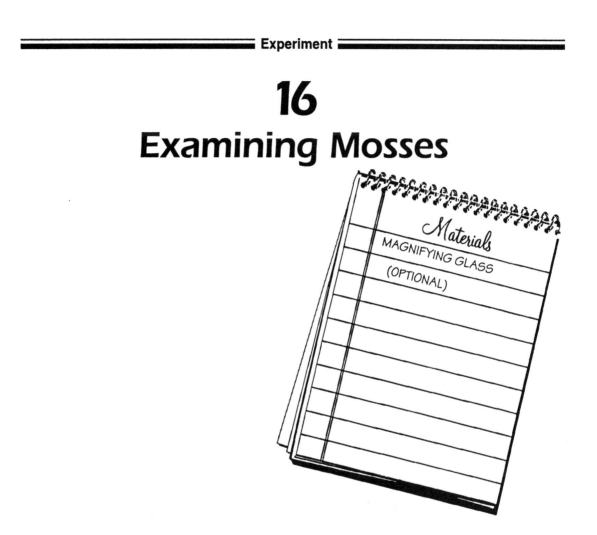

Materials

MAGNIFYING GLASS
(OPTIONAL)

Mosses are small feathery plants that grow in moist, shady areas. In this experiment you will try to find some moss.

PROCEDURE

1. Find a shady area. The base of a large tree is a good place.

2. Look for small plants that are fuzzy or feathery. This is probably a moss. See Fig. 16-1 for a drawing of the moss.

3. Examine the moss carefully. The part that you see is the part that catches the sunlight.

4. Return to look at the moss once a week for many weeks. You might see a tall stalk with a ball-like structure on the end. This structure will produce *spores*. Spores will produce a new plant (Fig. 16-1).

1 inch (2.5 cm)

Reproductive Structure

Fig. 16-1. *If you look closely at a moss plant (left), you may be able to see the part that forms spores (right).*

COMMENTS

Mosses do not have structures or tubes for moving water. They do not become large like other land plants. Mosses can grow on rocks. As they grow on the rocks, they help to break down the rocks so other plants can grow. Mosses provide food for many animals.

17
Plants at Different Seasons

Materials

- 4 PIECES OF STRING OR TAPE, EACH ABOUT 3 FEET (1 METER) LONG
- PAPER
- PENCIL
- CLEAR TAPE

In this experiment you will look for plants in an area at different times during the year. This experiment may take 30 minutes or more at each season.

PROCEDURE

1. Find an area outside to study. An area near woods or at the edge of your school yard is good.

2. Place the four pieces of string on the ground to form a square.

3. Count the number of different plants in the square (Fig. 17-1).

4. Take a leaf from each plant and tape it to the sheet of paper. Be careful not to touch any poison ivy or poison oak. Try to put all the different leaves on one or two sheets of paper. Label the sheet with the time of year you collected the leaves.

5. Return to this area at different times during the year, and repeat steps 2 to 4. Did you see different plants at different times?

6. Put your results on a graph like the one in Fig. 17-2.

Fig. 17-1. Examining plants in the marked area.

COMMENTS

Not all plants grow at the same time. Some plants need warmer temperatures than others to grow. Other plants need different amounts of light to grow well. You collected the leaves from the plants at different seasons. You did this so you could compare the growth at different seasons.

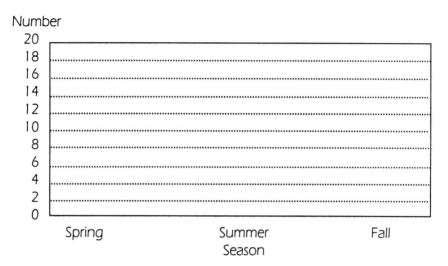

Fig. 17-2. *Graph for plants at different seasons.*

You may want to do this experiment for two years. You may see different plants in different years. Some seeds may have been carried by migrating animals. Scientists often study an area for many years. When different plants and animals do not reappear, scientists try to figure out why.

18

Effect of Light on Leaves

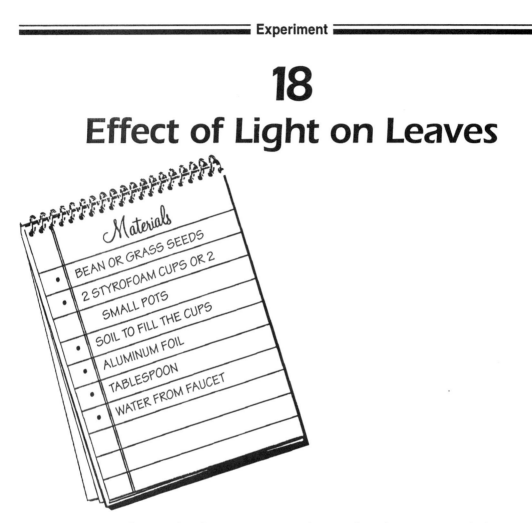

Materials

- BEAN OR GRASS SEEDS
- 2 STYROFOAM CUPS OR 2 SMALL POTS
- SOIL TO FILL THE CUPS
- ALUMINUM FOIL
- TABLESPOON
- WATER FROM FAUCET

You will see what happens to new leaves that don't get any light. This experiment will take 1 to 2 weeks.

PROCEDURE

1. Fill each cup one-half full with soil.

2. Place five seeds in each cup (Fig. 18-1).

3. Add 3 tablespoons of water to each cup.

4. Cover one cup with aluminum foil (Fig. 18-2).

5. Place cups on the window sill or on the counter.

6. Add 3 tablespoons of water each day to each cup. Be sure to replace the foil immediately after watering.

7. Compare the color of the leaves on each plant.

Fig. 18-1. *Planting the seeds.*

Fig. 18-2. *Making a dark enviroment.*

EXPLANATION

Light is necessary for plants to make the green color, *chlorophyll* (KLOR–O–FILL). Without light, leaves stay pale or white. The plants with the white leaves cannot make their own food, and eventually die. If you take the plant with white leaves, and put it in the light, the leaves will turn green.

You can do a similar experiment with a grown plant. Cover one or more of the leaves with aluminum foil, and wait 5 to 7 days. Remove the foil, and you will see that the covered leaves have lost most of their color.

19
Response of Plant to Touch

Materials

- WATER FROM FAUCET
- RULER
- TABLESPOON
- 8 TO 10 BEAN SEEDS OR 5 OR MORE SMALL TOMATO PLANTS
- 8 OR MORE STYROFOAM CUPS OR SMALL POTS
- POTTING SOIL TO FILL THE CUPS

Rubbing the stems of plants will affect how tall they grow. This experiment will take about 3 weeks. You can either start with small plants or you can start with seeds.

PROCEDURE

1. If you have small plants, go to step 4.

2. If you use bean seeds, soak the seeds in water for 6 hours; then plant the seeds, one seed per cup.

3. Water the seeds each day by adding 3 tablespoons of water to each cup.

4. After the first leaves appear, pick four plants that are the same height.

5. Label the cups "0," "10," "20," and "30."

6. Measure the height of each plant from the soil to the top of the stem. Record the measurements as "beginning."

7. Gently touch the stem between your thumb and forefinger (Fig. 19-1). Rub up and down the stem the indicated number of times (0, 10, 20, or 30).

Fig. 19-1. *Rub the stem of your plant.*

8. Repeat step 7 each day for 10 days. Be sure to keep the soil moist during this time (Fig. 19-2).

9. Measure the length of each stem from the soil to the tip of the stem. Record these numbers as "ending."

10. Put your results on a graph like the one in Fig. 19-3.

Fig. 19-2. Observe how rubbing affects the plant.

Height in cm

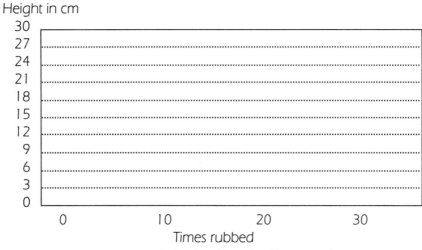

Times rubbed

Fig. 19-3. Graph for the effect of rubbing on plants.

EXPLANATION

Rubbing the stem causes the plant to make shorter, thicker stems. A similar response happens to plants outside when animals brush against them or when rain hits the plants. Thicker, shorter stems are less likely to break or fall over when they are hit or rubbed. Squash and cucumbers can also be used in this experiment.

20
Making Bushier Plants

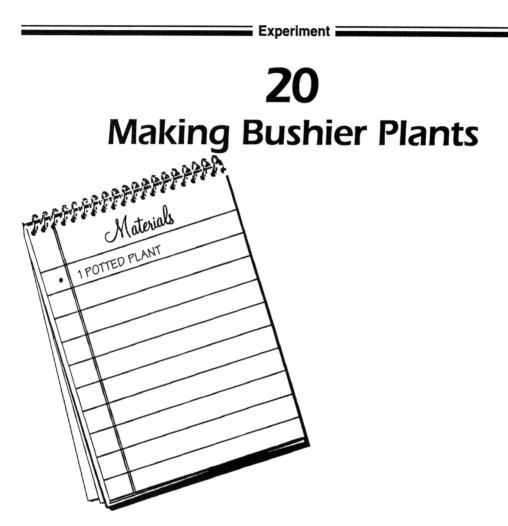

Materials

1 POTTED PLANT

You can make a plant have more leaves or become bushier. This experiment will take 1 or 2 weeks.

PROCEDURE

1. Pinch off the top 1 or 2 leaves from the plant (Fig. 20-1).

2. Count how many leaves remain on the plant.

3. Look at the plant each day. Water it if the soil seems to be dry. After about 1 week, you should begin to see new leaves forming further down on the stem.

Fig. 20-1. *Pinching the top of a plant.*

EXPLANATION

Most plants make a chemical that keeps leaves from forming everywhere except at the top of the stem. This chemical is made by the cells at the tip of the stem. The chemical moves down the stem and keeps other buds or leaves from forming. When you pinch off the top of the stem, you remove the chemical. New leaves can now form along the stem.

A similar thing happens when you trim bushes outside. New leaves appear beneath the top of the plant.

21

What Happens When You Plant a Seed

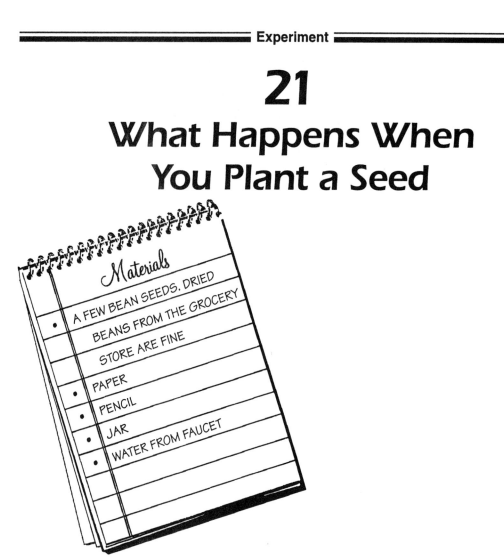

Materials

- A FEW BEAN SEEDS. DRIED BEANS FROM THE GROCERY STORE ARE FINE
- PAPER
- PENCIL
- JAR
- WATER FROM FAUCET

You always water seeds after you plant them. This experiment will show you what happens to seeds within the first day after you water them. This experiment requires a small amount of time on two days.

PROCEDURE

1. Place a seed on a sheet of paper. Trace around the seed with a pencil (Fig. 21-1).

2. Place a few seeds in a jar of water (Fig. 21-2).

3. Wait one day.

4. Remove a seed from the water and trace around it.

5. Compare the size of the seed before and after soaking.

Fig. 21-1. *Tracing the size of a seed.*

Fig. 21-2. *Soaking seeds in water.*

COMMENTS

The first thing that happens when you plant a seed is that it begins to take in water. This water causes the seed to swell. The extra water in the seed allows the seed to start growing.

22
The Effect of Saltwater on Seeds

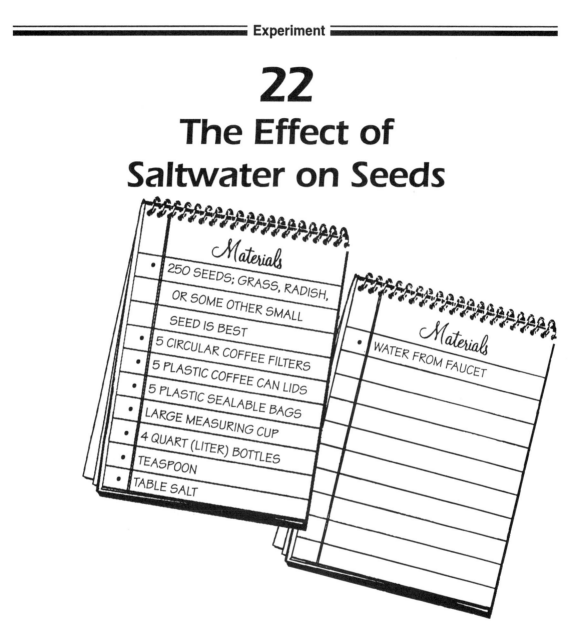

Materials
- 250 SEEDS; GRASS, RADISH, OR SOME OTHER SMALL SEED IS BEST
- 5 CIRCULAR COFFEE FILTERS
- 5 PLASTIC COFFEE CAN LIDS
- 5 PLASTIC SEALABLE BAGS
- LARGE MEASURING CUP
- 4 QUART (LITER) BOTTLES
- TEASPOON
- TABLE SALT

Materials
- WATER FROM FAUCET

You will see how saltwater influences the growth of seeds. This experiment will take 2 weeks.

PROCEDURE

1. Mix 1 teaspoon of salt in 1 quart (liter) of water (Fig. 22-1). Pour this solution into a jar labeled "1."

2. In a similar manner, prepare solutions that have 2, 3, and 4 teaspoons of salt in 1 quart (liter) of water. Pour each solution into separate labeled bottles.

3. Place the coffee filters on the plastic lids.

4. Place 50 seeds on each filter (Fig. 22-2).

5. Put 1 teaspoon of water onto one filter (Fig. 22-3).

6. Put the watered seeds into a plastic bag and seal it tightly. Label this bag "0" (Fig. 22-4).

7. Repeat steps 5 and 6 using a different salt solution for each filter. Label each bag with the number on the bottle you used.

8. Place all bags on the counter where they won't be disturbed. Wait 2 weeks.

9. After 2 weeks, count the number of seeds that have sprouted in each bag.

10. Place your results on a bar graph like the one shown in Fig. 22-5.

Fig. 22-1. *Mixing saltwater.*

Fig. 22-2. Put 50 seeds on each filter.

Fig. 22-3. Adding saltwater to seeds.

Fig. 22-4. Putting seeds into a bag.

Number growing

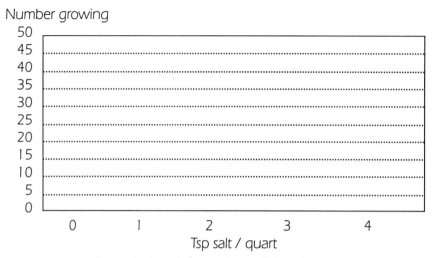

Tsp salt / quart

Fig. 22-5. Graph for seed growth in saltwater.

COMMENTS

Many of our lakes and streams now contain much salt. Some of this salt comes from *fertilizers* and other chemicals put into the soil. Too much salt can prevent some seeds or plants from growing.

Scientists are now doing this same experiment with many different kinds of plants. If seeds will grow in the presence of much salt, ocean water can be used to water some plants. Such watering would save fresh water for other purposes.

You can expand this experiment by using more than one type of seed. Or you can use ½ , 1, 1½, and 2 teaspoons of salt per quart (liter). For example, try different kinds of grasses.

23
Making a Plant Wilt

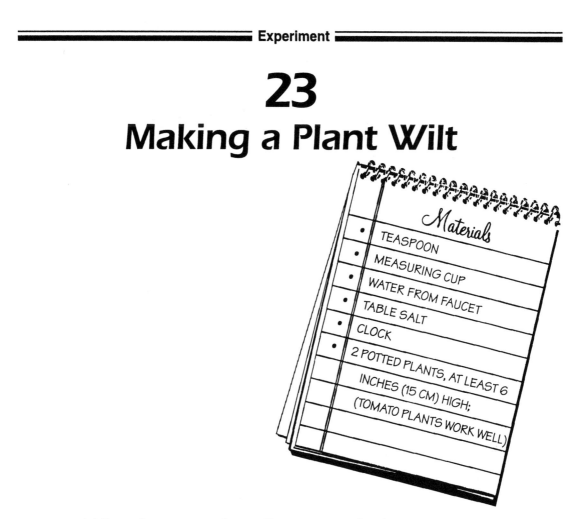

Materials

- TEASPOON
- MEASURING CUP
- WATER FROM FAUCET
- TABLE SALT
- CLOCK
- 2 POTTED PLANTS, AT LEAST 6 INCHES (15 CM) HIGH; (TOMATO PLANTS WORK WELL)

Adding saltwater to a plant will cause it to wilt. This experiment will take 60 minutes. It should be done outside or over the sink.

PROCEDURE

1. Put 2 ounces (60 ml) of water into a measuring cup.

2. Add 1½ teaspoons of salt to the water (Fig. 23-1). Stir until all the salt dissolves.

3. Slowly pour the saltwater onto the soil of one plant (Fig. 23-2).

4. Pour 2 ounces (60 ml) of water onto the soil of the other plant.

5. Look at the plants every 10 minutes for the next hour. At some point, the plant in saltwater will begin to wilt.

6. Once the plant wilts, add about 3 ounces (90 ml) of water (NOT SALTWATER) to the soil of the wilted plant. Be sure the plant is over the sink.

Fig. 23-1. *Making saltwater.*

Fig. 23-2. *Pouring saltwater on a plant.*

EXPLANATION

Water moves from an area with few particles to an area with many particles. The soil with saltwater had more particles than the *cells* of the plant. Water left this plant to go to the soil. When plant cells lose water they become floppy, like a balloon losing air, and the plant wilts.

The heavy use of fertilizer on farms is both good and bad. The chemicals in the fertilizers help the plant grow, but these extra chemicals stay in the soil. When plants are planted, there may be too many chemicals in the soil. These plants will wilt and not grow well. The extra fertilizer acts like the salt in this experiment. The soil of some farms is now too salty for some plants to grow.

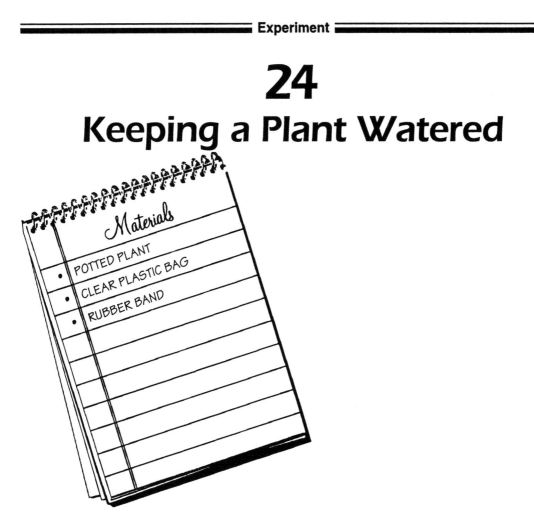

24
Keeping a Plant Watered

Materials

- POTTED PLANT
- CLEAR PLASTIC BAG
- RUBBER BAND

You can keep a plant watered without adding water to the soil. This experiment will take 2 or 3 days.

PROCEDURE

1. Place the plastic bag over the plant (Fig. 24-1).

2. Put the rubber band around the pot so that the bag is held in place.

3. Look at the bag every 3 hours. You will see drops of water beginning to form on the inside of the bag (Fig. 24-2).

Fig. 24-1. *Placing a bag over the plant.*

Fig. 24-2. *Watch water drops form inside the bag.*

EXPLANATION

Water in plants evaporates through tiny openings in the leaves. Usually this water goes into the air. The plastic bag kept the water from going into the air.

You might think it is bad for plants to lose water through their leaves. It is, but it is also necessary to help the plant move the water from the roots to the leaves. Water leaving the leaves creates a *suction* that pulls water up from the soil.

You can use this experiment when you go on vacation. Cover your house plants with plastic bags. The drops of water that form will drop back into the soil and keep the plant moist.

25
Growing Seeds Together—Part 1

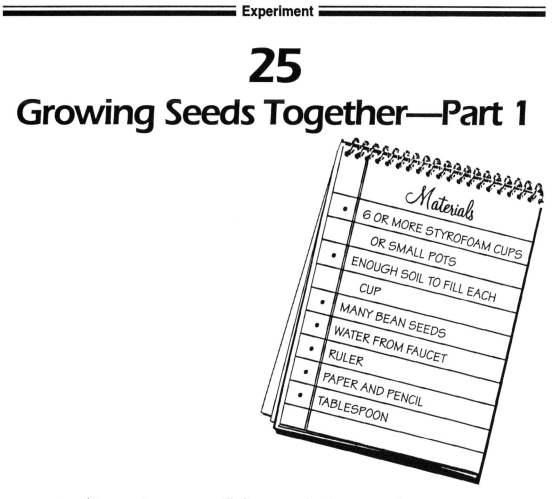

Materials

- 6 OR MORE STYROFOAM CUPS OR SMALL POTS
- ENOUGH SOIL TO FILL EACH CUP
- MANY BEAN SEEDS
- WATER FROM FAUCET
- RULER
- PAPER AND PENCIL
- TABLESPOON

In this experiment you will discover what happens when too many seeds of the same kind are planted in the same space. The experiment takes 3 weeks.

PROCEDURE

1. Label the cups "1," "2," "3," "4," "6," "10."

2. Fill each cup with dirt.

3. Plant the number of seeds indicated on the cup. For example, put four seeds in the cup marked 4. Try to spread the seeds evenly in the cup (Fig. 25-1).

4. Add 3 tablespoons of water to each cup.

5. Place cups in a sunny area where they will not be disturbed. A windowsill is a good place.

6. Each day, water the soil with 3 tablespoons of water. Do this every day for 3 weeks.

7. After 3 weeks, measure the height of the tallest plant in each cup. Measure from the soil to the top of the stem.

8. Put your results on a bar graph like the one in Fig. 25-2.

Fig. 25-1. Planting different amounts of seeds.

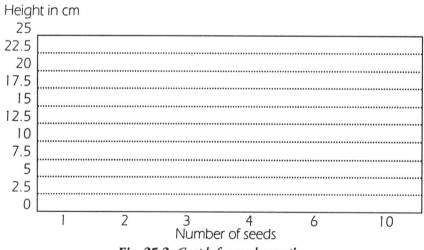

Fig. 25-2. Graph for seed growth.

EXPLANATION

You probably observed that the plants in each cup were different sizes. Each plant needs a certain amount of space for good growth. When plants get too close together, they do not have enough space for their roots. They can't get food, so they don't grow as well. If you plant a garden, it is important that the plants are far enough apart.

26
Growing Seeds Together—Part 2

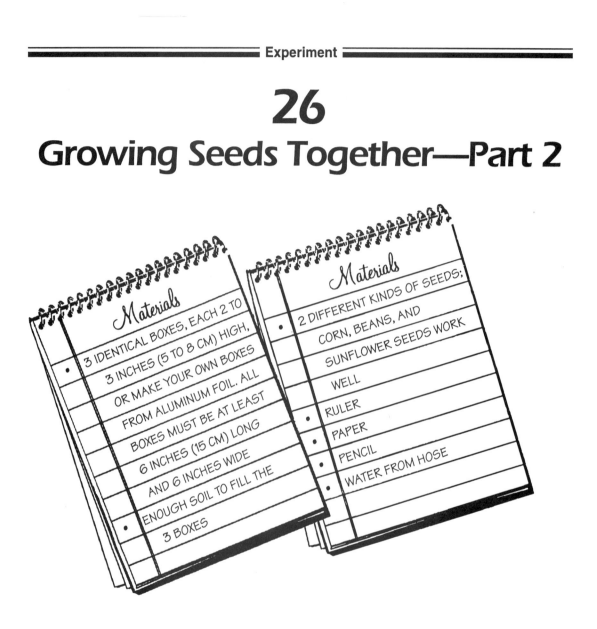

Materials

- 3 IDENTICAL BOXES, EACH 2 TO 3 INCHES (5 TO 8 CM) HIGH, OR MAKE YOUR OWN BOXES FROM ALUMINUM FOIL. ALL BOXES MUST BE AT LEAST 6 INCHES (15 CM) LONG AND 6 INCHES WIDE
- ENOUGH SOIL TO FILL THE 3 BOXES

Materials

- 2 DIFFERENT KINDS OF SEEDS; CORN, BEANS, AND SUNFLOWER SEEDS WORK WELL
- RULER
- PAPER
- PENCIL
- WATER FROM HOSE

In the last experiment, you grew the same kind of seeds close to each other. In this experiment you will see how well different kinds of seeds will grow together. This experiment will take 4 to 6 weeks.

PROCEDURE

1. Fill the three boxes with dirt.

2. With the ruler, mark spaces 4 cm apart for the seeds (Fig. 26-1).

3. In one box, plant nine seeds of one kind. Label the box with the kind of seeds you used.

4. In the second box, plant nine seeds of the second kind. Label the box with the kind of seeds you used.

5. Plant five seeds of one kind and four of the other in the third box. Label this box "Mix." The same kinds of seeds should not be placed next to one another (Fig. 26-2).

6. Place all three boxes outside in the sun.

7. Moisten the soil with water from the hose.

8. Keep the soil moist by watering each box every day.

9. Once the seeds sprout, measure the height of the tallest and shortest plants in each box once a week for four weeks. Write down the heights.

10. Compare the heights of the plants in the three boxes. Did one plant grow less in the mix than it did alone?

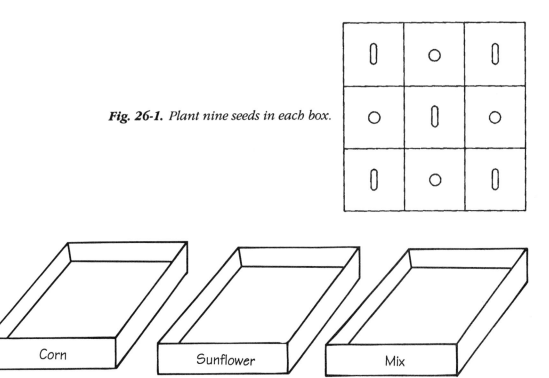

Fig. 26-1. Plant nine seeds in each box.

Fig. 26-2. Label the boxes.

EXPLANATION

Some plants make chemicals that keep other types of plants from growing well. Some other plants make chemicals that allow different plants to grow better. The boxes with only one kind of seed were used for comparison with the boxes of mixed plants grown together.

27
Growing Plants from Seeds You Throw Out

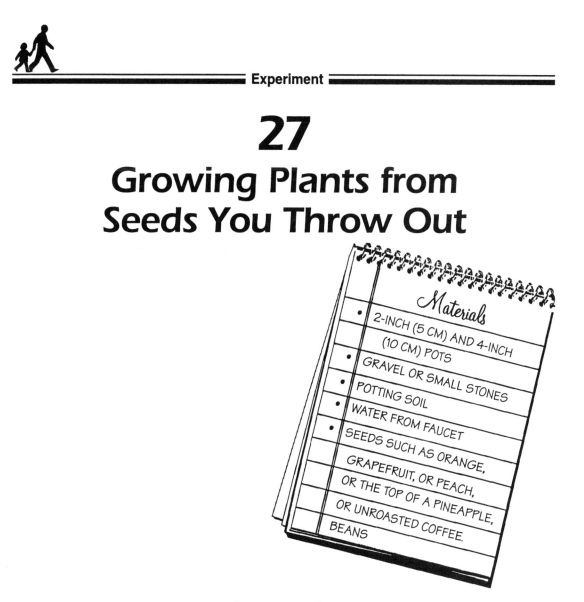

Materials

- 2-INCH (5 CM) AND 4-INCH (10 CM) POTS
- GRAVEL OR SMALL STONES
- POTTING SOIL
- WATER FROM FAUCET
- SEEDS SUCH AS ORANGE, GRAPEFRUIT, OR PEACH, OR THE TOP OF A PINEAPPLE, OR UNROASTED COFFEE BEANS

You can grow some nice plants or trees from seeds you usually throw out. Some seeds will take many weeks before they start to grow.

PROCEDURE

For any seed, fill the pot a quarter full with gravel, then cover the gravel with soil to fill the pot. Following are specific instructions for different kinds of seeds.

Pineapple

1. Slice off the top of the pineapple. Leave about ½ inch (1 cm) of the fruit.

2. Barely cover the fruit with soil in a shallow pot (Fig. 27-1).

3. Put the plant on a windowsill and water it as needed.

Fig. 27-1. Plant the top of a pineapple.

Orange, lemon, or grapefruit

1. Wash the seeds with water.

2. Place seeds on a paper towel and allow to dry for 4 to 6 days.

3. Plant two or three seeds 1 inch (2.5 cm) deep in soil (Fig. 27-2).

4. Keep the soil moist.

5. In 4 to 6 weeks new plants will appear.

6. When the plants are 4 inches (10 cm) high, put each plant in a separate pot.

7. Water these trees as needed.

Peaches

1. Wash the seed and allow to dry on a paper towel for 4 to 6 days.

2. Plant the peach seed in a 4 inch (10 cm) pot, 1 inch (2.5 cm) below the surface.

3. Keep the soil moist.

Fig. 27-2. Planting a grapefruit seed.

Coffee

1. Obtain some unroasted coffee beans from a coffee store.

2. Put four to six beans in a 2-inch (5 cm) pot so that they are 1 inch (2.5 cm) below the surface.

3. Keep the soil moist.

COMMENTS

When you finish this experiment you will have grown some nice trees from some seeds you usually throw out. You will need to put the trees into bigger pots every two or three years. To make your tree bushier, pinch off the tip of the main stem every 2 to 3 months. (See Experiment 20).

28
Planting a Vegetable Garden

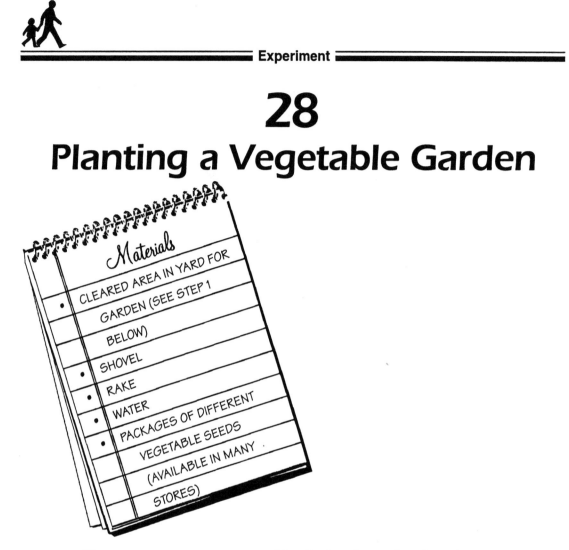

Materials

- CLEARED AREA IN YARD FOR GARDEN (SEE STEP 1 BELOW)
- SHOVEL
- RAKE
- WATER
- PACKAGES OF DIFFERENT VEGETABLE SEEDS (AVAILABLE IN MANY STORES)

You can grow your own vegetables. In 2 or 3 months after planting, you will have vegetables to eat.

PROCEDURE

1. Decide how big you want your garden to be. You can grow two or three kinds of vegetables in a space 3 feet (1 meter) × 10 feet (3 meters) or 5 feet (1.5 meters) × 6 feet (2 meters).

2. Dig up the soil to loosen the dirt. You may want to ask an adult to help you do this.

3. Smooth the dirt with a rake.

4. Decide what vegetables you wish to grow. Beans, squash, and cucumbers grow fast and produce many vegetables. Spinach and lettuce are good choices to plant for the early spring.

5. Plant the seeds according to the directions on the package (Fig. 28-1).

6. Water the soil every day with a hose or watering can.

7. After the plants start to grow, keep the weeds away by pulling them out of the ground.

8. Water the plants every other day, or every day if there has been no rain.

9. Pick the vegetables when they are ripe.

Fig. 28-1. *Planting a vegetable garden.*

COMMENTS

You can also use small plants instead of seeds. Tomatoes and eggplant are good choices. If you have room and can wait about 3 months, try planting pumpkin seeds. When the pumpkins appear, keep only two pumpkins per vine.

29
Planting a Flower Garden

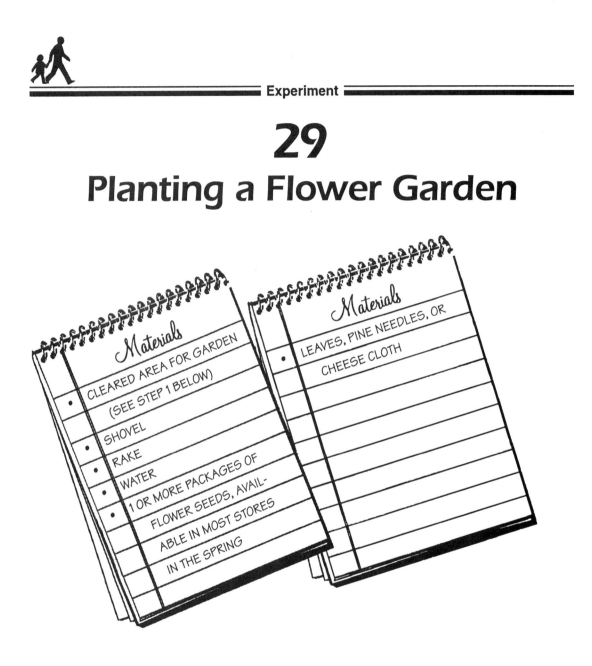

Materials

- CLEARED AREA FOR GARDEN (SEE STEP 1 BELOW)
- SHOVEL
- RAKE
- WATER
- 1 OR MORE PACKAGES OF FLOWER SEEDS, AVAILABLE IN MOST STORES IN THE SPRING

Materials

- LEAVES, PINE NEEDLES, OR CHEESE CLOTH

You can make a flower garden that will have flowers for many months. It will take 4 to 6 weeks before you have flowers.

PROCEDURE

1. Decide how big you want your garden.

2. Dig up this size space with a shovel. You may need an adult to help with this.

3. Smooth the dirt out with a rake.

4. Plant the seeds evenly all over the cleared area.

5. Cover the seeds with about ½ inch (1 cm) of dirt, or with leaves, pine needles, or cheese cloth. The covering will prevent birds from eating too many of the seeds.

6. Water the soil with a spray of water. The soil should be moist, but not soaking wet.

7. Repeat step number 6 every day for one to two weeks.

8. Look for plants to appear in about two weeks (Fig. 29-1).

9. When the plants are about 3 inches (7 to 8 cm) tall, remove some of the plants that are close together.

10. Wait for flowers to appear.

Fig. 29-1. *Planting flower seeds.*

COMMENTS

You can cut some of the flowers and put them in a vase. Most plants will make flowers for 2 to 3 months. Let some of the flowers dry and the seeds fall to the ground. The seeds will grow next year and you will have another flower garden.

30
Making Colored Flowers

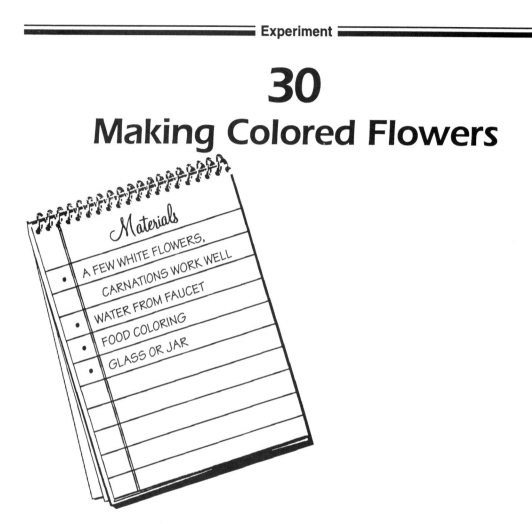

Materials

- A FEW WHITE FLOWERS, CARNATIONS WORK WELL
- WATER FROM FAUCET
- FOOD COLORING
- GLASS OR JAR

You can make different colored flowers. This experiment will take about one day.

PROCEDURE

1. Fill the glass or jar one-half full with water.

2. Add 5 to 10 drops of food coloring to the water and mix.

3. Place the stem of a flower in the colored water (Fig. 30-1).

4. Keep the flower in the water overnight, or until the flower begins to change color.

Fig. 30-1. *Place flower in colored water.*

EXPLANATION

The stems of plants have many small tubes through which water moves. The water and the food coloring move up the stem to the flower, and the flower changes color. Florists use this method to make flowers with unusual colors that do not appear in nature.

Part III
Earth Science
Experiments

The world around you is made up of air, water, and land. The air changes temperature and also acquires water from rivers and lakes. The water forms clouds and sometimes returns to earth as rain, snow, or hail. The sun heats the air and the water, but water is heated more slowly than air.

Both the air and the water are not as clean as they seem. They contain many small particles. In this chapter, you will study many different things about air, water, and land. You will see some of the particles in the air and also make your own rainbow.

31
Making Your Own Rainbow

Materials

- HOSE ATTACHED TO OUTSIDE FAUCET
- NOZZLE TO MAKE A FINE SPRAY OF WATER

You can make a rainbow outside on a sunny day.

PROCEDURE

1. Place nozzle on hose.

2. Turn on the water and adjust nozzle so a fine spray of water comes out.

3. Stand with your back to the sun.

4. Spray the water away from you, and look for the rainbow near the water. You may have to move the nozzle up and down (Fig. 31-1).

Fig. 31-1. *Spraying water to make a rainbow.*

EXPLANATION

Light from the sun is made up of many different colors of light. As this light passes through water, each color of light is bent differently. Individual colors now appear. When you see a rainbow in the sky, the rainbow is always in the opposite direction from the sun. The sunlight passes through many water drops, and the light is bent. The rainbow that you see may be off to the edge of the spray.

32
Measuring Shadows

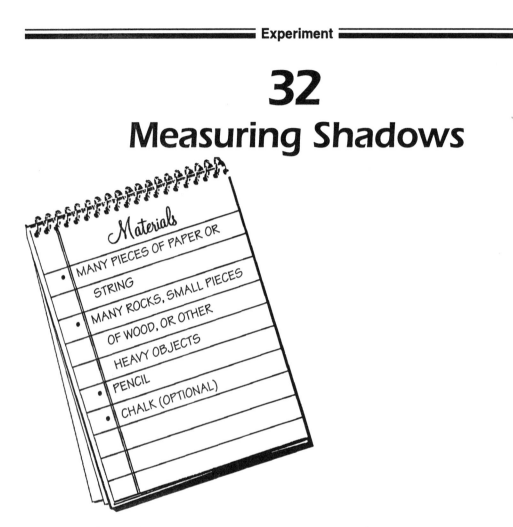

Materials

- MANY PIECES OF PAPER OR STRING
- MANY ROCKS, SMALL PIECES OF WOOD, OR OTHER HEAVY OBJECTS
- PENCIL
- CHALK (OPTIONAL)

The shadow your body makes changes at different times of the day. This experiment goes on all day.

PROCEDURE

1. Go outside and place a sheet of paper on the ground. Place weights on the paper so it won't blow away. Or, you can stand on the sidewalk and mark where you are standing with chalk.

2. Ask a friend to mark where the head of your shadow is. Write the time on the paper or sidewalk (Fig. 32-1).

3. Two or three hours later, go outside again and stand in the same place.

4. Mark the position of the head of your shadow.

5. Repeat steps 3 and 4 one or two more times during the day. Did your shadow stay in the same place? Was it the same size?

Fig. 32-1. *Measuring a shadow.*

EXPLANATION

A shadow forms because light does not pass through your body. The earth spins so the position of the sun changes throughout the day. Shadows will be shorter when the sun is almost overhead.

You can do a similar experiment inside with a can and a flashlight. Move the flashlight to different places, and look at the shadow of the can.

33

How Clean Is the Air?

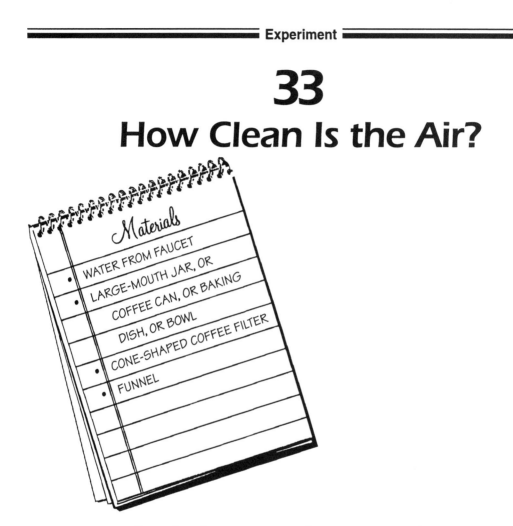

Materials

- WATER FROM FAUCET
- LARGE-MOUTH JAR, OR COFFEE CAN, OR BAKING DISH, OR BOWL
- CONE-SHAPED COFFEE FILTER
- FUNNEL

You will see that the air is not as clean as you may think it is. This experiment will take 2 to 4 days.

PROCEDURE

1. Fill the jar about one-half full with water.

2. Set the jar outside for 2–3 days.

3. Put the coffee filter in the funnel.

4. Pour the water through the filter (Fig. 33-1). If you do this step indoors, be sure to hold the filter over the sink.

5. Examine the filter. You should see many things on the filter.

Fig. 33-1. *Pouring water through a filter.*

EXPLANATION

The filter probably turned dark. Particles of dirt, smoke, and pollen that are in the air fell into the water. You trapped these particles on the paper. These are only the large particles that are in the air; many more smaller particles are also in the air. If you have a magnifying glass, use it to examine the particles on the filter paper.

34
Cleaning Up Water

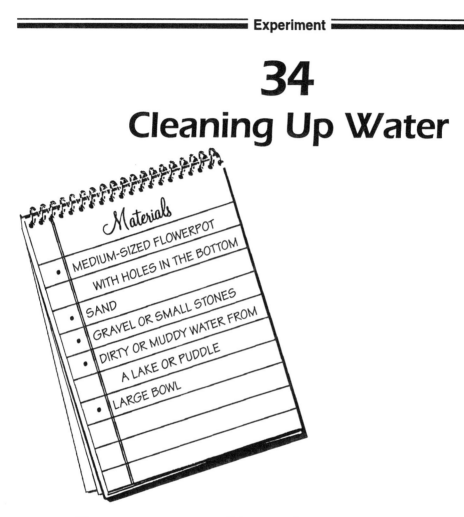

Materials

- MEDIUM-SIZED FLOWERPOT WITH HOLES IN THE BOTTOM
- SAND
- GRAVEL OR SMALL STONES
- DIRTY OR MUDDY WATER FROM A LAKE OR PUDDLE
- LARGE BOWL

You can remove many of the particles in water.

PROCEDURE

1. Fill the pot one-half full with small stones.

2. Fill the rest of the pot with sand (Fig. 34-1).

3. Hold the pot over a bowl.

4. Slowly pour the "dirty water" into the pot.

5. Observe the water that enters the bowl. Compare it to the water you poured in.

Fig. 34-1. Place sand and gravel in a pot.

EXPLANATION

The sand acts like a filter (see Experiment 33) to trap the particles that are in the water. As the water slowly moves through the sand, it loses particles. The stones allow the water to leave the pot at a faster rate.

The filtering systems of most swimming pools use this method. Water from the pool enters the filter from the top, flows through the sand and gravel, and finally returns to the pool.

35
Catching a Raindrop

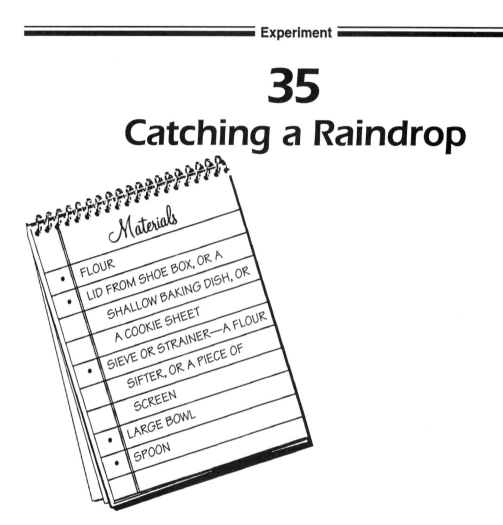

Materials

- FLOUR
- LID FROM SHOE BOX, OR A SHALLOW BAKING DISH, OR A COOKIE SHEET
- SIEVE OR STRAINER—A FLOUR SIFTER, OR A PIECE OF SCREEN
- LARGE BOWL
- SPOON

You can keep a raindrop.

PROCEDURE

1. Pour some flour into the shoe box lid so it is about ½ inch (1 cm) deep.

2. With a spoon, spread out flour so the surface is even.

3. Place the lid outside in the rain for about 5 minutes (Fig. 35-1).

4. Pour the flour through the sieve (Fig. 35-2). Place a bowl under the sieve to collect the flour, or pour over a sink.

6. Look for small lumps in the sieve.

Fig. 35-1. *Placing flour outside.*

Fig. 35-2. *Pouring flour through a sieve.*

EXPLANATION

The raindrops make the *particles* of the flour stick together to form small lumps.

36
Cutting a Hailstone

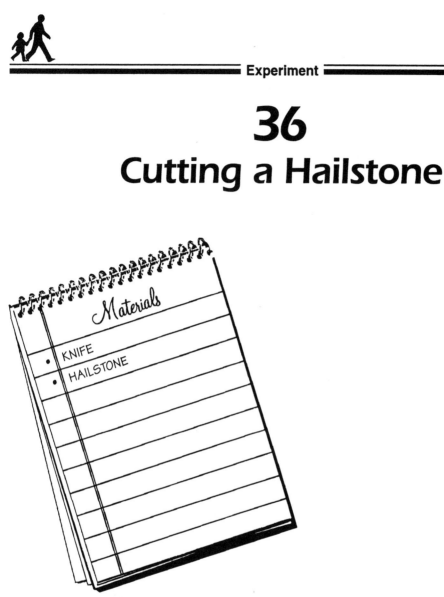

Materials

- KNIFE
- HAILSTONE

You will examine the inside of a hailstone, if you can find one.

PROCEDURE

1. If there is a hailstorm, try to gather a few hailstones and quickly bring them inside.

2. Ask an adult to cut the stone in half (Fig. 36-1).

3. Examine the inside of the stone. You may be surprised to see that it is in layers (Fig. 36-2).

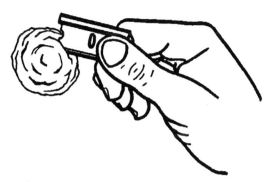

Fig. 36-1. *Have an adult cut a hailstone in half for you.*

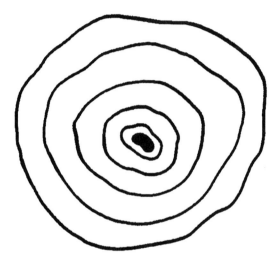

Fig. 36-2. *The inside of a hailstone is in layers.*

EXPLANATION

Hail is formed by raindrops freezing many times. As the rain falls, it is frozen, and then pushed higher into the sky. More water attaches to the stone, and this is also frozen. This process occurs many times. The result is a hailstone that looks like a jawbreaker candy with many layers.

37
Making a Cloud

You can make your own cloud in a jar.

PROCEDURE

1. Have an adult light a match and put the burning match inside a jar (Fig. 37-1).

2. After the match is out, hold the jar and breathe into it (Fig. 37-2).

3. Allow the jar to cool.

4. See what happens inside the jar.

Fig. 37-1. *Have an adult light a match in a jar.*

Fig. 37-2. *Blowing into a jar.*

EXPLANATION

Clouds need two things to form: small particles in the air and warm, moist air. Burning the match put small particles into the air. Your breath provided the warm, moist air. As the jar cooled, water condensed around the tiny particles.

Particles are always in the air. When clouds do not form in the sky, the air is very dry.

38
Recording Outside Temperatures

Materials

- 1 OUTDOOR THERMOMETER
- PAPER
- PENCIL

You will keep a record of outside temperatures for a month.

PROCEDURE

1. Place thermometer outside where it will not be disturbed.

2. In the morning (about 8:00) and in the afternoon (about 4:00), write down the temperature (Fig. 38-1).

3. Repeat step 2 every day for a month. Be sure to record the temperature at the same times each day.

4. Put the temperatures on a bar graph.

Daily temperatures

Date	Morning	Afternoon	Date	Morning	Afternoon
1			17		
2			18		
3			19		
4			20		
5			21		
6			22		
7			23		
8			24		
9			25		
10			26		
11			27		
12			28		
13			29		
14			30		
15			31		
16					

Fig. 38-1. *Chart for recording temperatures.*

COMMENTS

The weather service keeps a record of temperatures each day. Some days the temperature changes alot from morning to afternoon. On other days, it stays almost the same. Clouds and seasons will affect the temperature during the day.

39
Temperature Inside
a Closed Container

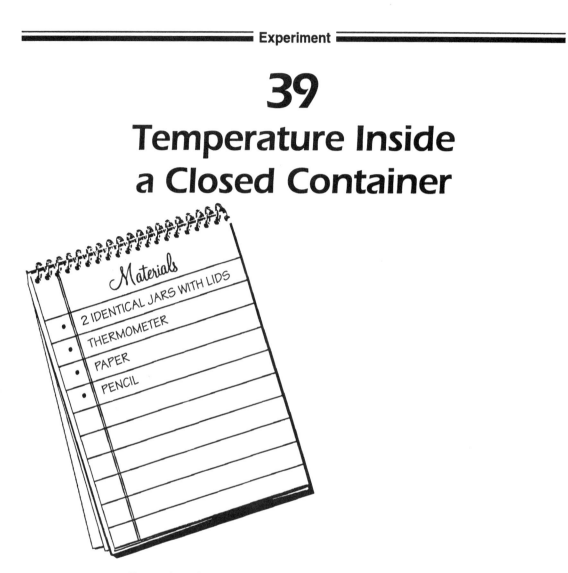

Materials

- 2 IDENTICAL JARS WITH LIDS
- THERMOMETER
- PAPER
- PENCIL

You will see that the temperature inside a closed jar gets very hot. This experiment will take about 2 hours.

PROCEDURE

1. Place the jars outside in the hot sun (Fig. 39-1).

2. Measure the temperature in each jar. Write them down. Call these the "starting temperatures" (Fig. 39-2).

3. Put the lid on one of the jars.

4. Wait 60 minutes and measure the temperatures again. Measure the temperature in the closed jar first. Record the temperatures. Call these the "ending temperatures."

5. Put your results on a graph like the one in Fig. 39-3.

Fig. 39-1. *Setting containers outside in the sun.*

Fig. 39-2. *Measuring and recording temperatures.*

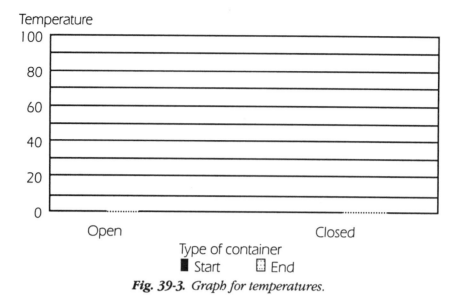

Fig. 39-3. *Graph for temperatures.*

EXPLANATION

The sun heats the air in both jars, but the air in the closed jar cannot leave the jar. The air in the closed jar gets much warmer than the air in the open jar.

A closed car behaves the same way as a closed jar. It becomes very hot sitting in the sun. It is not wise or safe to leave pets in a closed car for more than five minutes during the summer. Even with the windows partially opened, the temperature rises so much that a pet could get too hot and even die.

40
The Effect of
Color on Temperature

Materials

- 1 SHEET BLACK CONSTRUCTION PAPER
- 1 SHEET WHITE CONSTRUCTION PAPER
- 2 JARS THE SAME SIZE
- TAPE
- WATER FROM FAUCET
- LARGE BOWL
- THERMOMETER
- SCISSORS

You will determine which color makes the temperature change more. This experiment will take 1 to 2 hours.

PROCEDURE

1. Fill a large bowl with water and let this bowl set on the counter for about 1 hour.

2. Cut a strip of paper so that it will cover the whole jar.

3. Wrap the black paper around one jar and tape the paper in place. Do the same thing for the white paper. The paper should cover the whole jar (Fig. 40-1).

4. Fill each jar with water from the bowl.

5. Place both jars in a sunny window or in a sunny spot in the yard.

6. After an hour, measure the temperature in each jar (Fig. 40-2).

Fig. 40-1. *Cover two jars with different colored paper.*

Fig. 40-2. *Measuring and recording temperatures.*

EXPLANATION

Black objects absorb light and heat. White objects reflect light and heat. The heat absorbed by the black paper traveled to the water in the jar and made the water hotter. It is not a good idea to wear black or dark clothing in the summer because the black will absorb lots of heat and make you hotter.

41

How Hot Do Different Things Become?

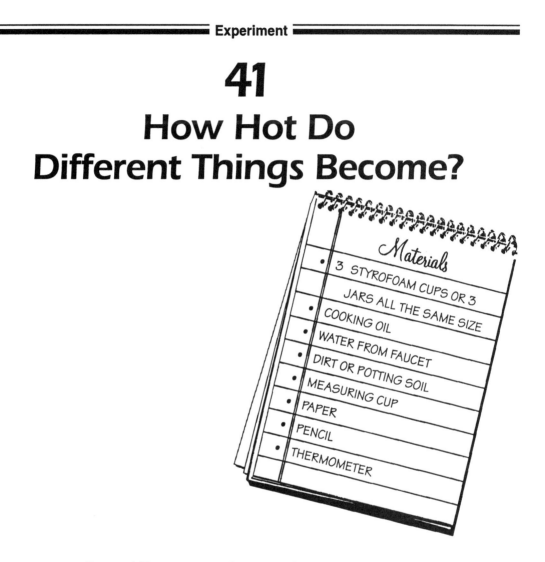

Materials

- 3 STYROFOAM CUPS OR 3 JARS ALL THE SAME SIZE
- COOKING OIL
- WATER FROM FAUCET
- DIRT OR POTTING SOIL
- MEASURING CUP
- PAPER
- PENCIL
- THERMOMETER

You will test different materials to see how much heat they gain while setting in the sun. This experiment will take about 2 hours.

PROCEDURE

1. Fill one cup with 4 ounces (100 ml) of water.

2. Fill a second cup with 5 ounces (125 ml) of cooking oil.

3. Fill a third cup with 12 ounces (350 ml) of dirt.

4. Allow all the cups to sit on the counter for 30 minutes.

5. Measure and record the temperature of each cup.

6. Place all three cups outside in the sun for 1 hour.

7. Measure and record the temperature in each cup after 1 hour in the sun (Fig. 41-1).

Which material showed the largest increase in temperature?

Fig. 41-1. *Measuring temperatures.*

EXPLANATION

Different materials absorb different amounts of heat. Water is a good material for living things because it can absorb much heat without having its temperature rise much.

Many portable heaters have oil inside of them. The oil will get quite hot, and then slowly give off the heat to the surrounding room.

You may want to expand this experiment. After the cups have sat in the sun, bring them inside. Wait 15 to 20 minutes and measure the temperatures again. The temperature of which material decreased the most?

42
How Much Water Will Soils Hold?

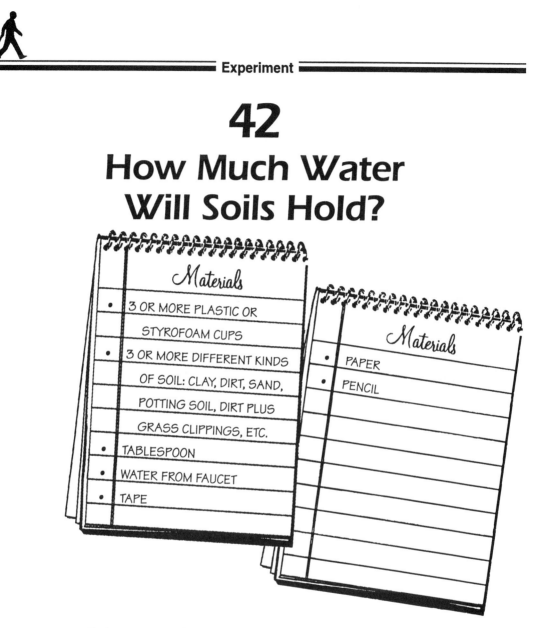

Materials

- 3 OR MORE PLASTIC OR STYROFOAM CUPS
- 3 OR MORE DIFFERENT KINDS OF SOIL: CLAY, DIRT, SAND, POTTING SOIL, DIRT PLUS GRASS CLIPPINGS, ETC.
- TABLESPOON
- WATER FROM FAUCET
- TAPE

Materials

- PAPER
- PENCIL

You will determine which type of soil holds the most water. This experiment will take about 30 minutes.

PROCEDURE

1. With the pencil, punch three holes in the bottom of each cup (Fig. 42-1).

2. Label each cup with the kind of soil to be used.

107

3. Fill each cup with a different kind of soil. If you use soil and grass clippings, mix equal amounts of each item in a bowl, then fill the cup.

4. Do the rest of the experiment outside or hold the cup over the sink. Add 1 tablespoon of water (Fig. 42-2).

5. Count to 15 and then add another spoonful of water.

6. Repeat step 5 until water drips out the bottom of the cup.

7. Write down the number of spoonfuls you used.

8. Repeat steps 4 to 7 for each type of soil.

9. Put your results on a graph like the one in Fig. 42-3.

Which soil held the most water? Which soil held the least water?

Fig. 42-1. Making holes in a cup.

EXPLANATION

Different kinds of soil hold different amounts of water. The size of particles in the soil affects how much water the soil will hold. Plants in different soils will need to be watered more or less depending on the type of soil.

Fig. 42-2. *Putting water into cups.*

Spoonfuls

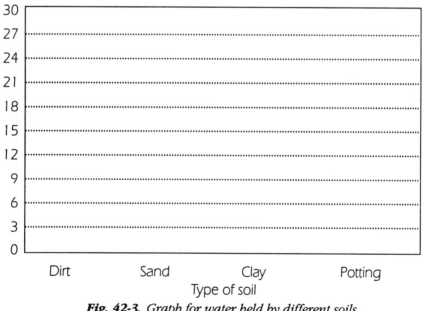

Type of soil

Fig. 42-3. *Graph for water held by different soils.*

43

What Grows in New Soil?

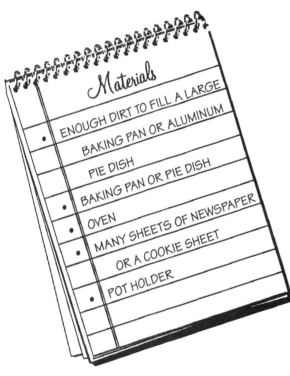

Materials

- ENOUGH DIRT TO FILL A LARGE BAKING PAN OR ALUMINUM PIE DISH
- BAKING PAN OR PIE DISH
- OVEN
- MANY SHEETS OF NEWSPAPER OR A COOKIE SHEET
- POT HOLDER

Different plants will begin to grow in fresh soil. This experiment will take many weeks.

PROCEDURE

1. Ask an adult to turn on the oven to about 300 degrees (150 degrees Celsius).

2. Spread out the dirt on newspaper or cookie sheet. Make the layer of dirt very thin.

3. Place the dirt in the heated oven for 3 to 4 hours.

4. Turn off the oven.

5. Use a potholder to remove the cookie sheet or newspaper from the oven.

6. Allow the dirt to cool.

7. Fill the pan with the baked dirt.

8. Place the pan outside (Fig. 43-1).

9. Look at the dirt once a week for many weeks. Has anything started to grow in the dirt?

10. Make a list of how many different plants grew in the dirt.

You may want to do this experiment at two different times, once in the spring and once in the summer.

Fig. 43-1. *Putting baked soil outside.*

COMMENTS

You heated the soil to kill everything, like seeds, that was present in the soil. Once the dirt was outside, new seeds landed in the soil and began to grow. The wind may have blown some seeds into the dirt. Birds or insects may have carried other seeds to the dirt.

Scientists do this type of experiment when fires, volcanoes, or floods destroy an area of land. One area that is being studied in this way is in Washington State near the volcano Mount St. Helens. This volcano erupted in 1981 and destroyed many plants.

Fires may destroy large forests, but sometimes fires are necessary. The seeds of some pine trees need a very high temperature to start growing.

44
Twirling a Bucket Without Spilling the Water

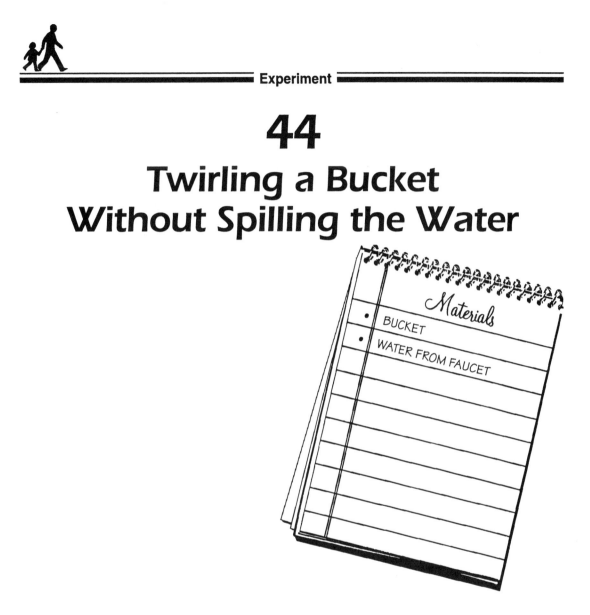

Materials
- BUCKET
- WATER FROM FAUCET

If you take a bucket of water and swing it around your head, the water will stay in the bucket.

PROCEDURE

1. Fill the bucket with water.

2. Quickly spin the bucket in a circle like a windmill. The water will stay in the bucket (Fig. 44-1).

3. Try different speeds of spinning to determine when the water begins to spill out.

Fig. 44-1. *Swinging the bucket.*

EXPLANATION

When anything spins in a circle, a force tends to push things to the outside of the circle. When the bucket is overhead and moving, the force is strong enough to keep the water from spilling out.

Appendix
A Scavenger Hunt

On a scavenger hunt, you try to find as many items as possible from a list of items. You can do one alone or with a group of friends. You can use the lists below, or you or your parents can make up another list.

The next time you are in a park or the woods, or on your school grounds, stop and look at all the things around you. You will be surprised how many interesting things are right in front of you. All you have to do is look.

The items on the two lists below are things you probably used or found while you were doing some of the experiments.

List 1

- 3 different kinds of seeds

- pine needles

- stem with alternate leaves

- yellow flower

- purple flower

- feather from a bird

- a beetle

- animal that is not an insect

- moss

- something man-made

- flower with only male parts

- grasshopper

- animal that is attracted to light

List 2

- 3 different kinds of seeds

- leaf (from tree that loses leaves)

- stem with opposite leaves

- white flower

- red or blue flower

- feather from a bird

- a beetle

- animal that is not an insect

- mushroom

- something left by a human

- flower with only female parts

- butterfly

- animal that prefers the dark

Glossary

alternate leaves Arrangement of leaves on stem where leaves are not next to each other on the stem.

cell Smallest unit of all living things. A plant or animal may contain billions of cells.

chlorophyll In plants, green chemical that traps sunlight and allows plants to make food from the sun.

cocoon In some animals, a hard case that will give rise to a butterfly or moth.

condense To form water from a gas.

development Process of going from one cell to an organism with many different parts.

fertilizer Chemicals added to soil to help plants grow better.

filter Device, often made of paper, that traps large particles but allows smaller ones to pass through.

flexible Easily bent or capable of changing shape.

florist Person or business that sells flowers.

larva Caterpillar or worm-like form of some insects; it crawls on land and eventually changes into the adult insects that you know.

maggot Another term for larva.

migrate To move from one area to another area that is far away.

nectar Sweet substance made by flowers to attract and feed insects.

pollen Small particles made by male part of plant. They travel in the wind and on the legs of animals.

prediction A guess about what will happen.

response Reaction to some type of signal.

sieve Screen material used to separate large and small particles.

solution Uniform mixture of a solid in a liquid; the liquid is clear and seems to have nothing in it.

spore Very small reproductive structure produced by molds, bacteria, and some plants; similar to a seed. Can tolerate very dry areas for a long time.

suction A force made by sucking, such as a vacuum cleaner.

thermometer Device for measuring temperature.

wilt To sag or become floppy because of loss of water.

Index